Transitions
In
Retirement

Part 1
Preparation For Retirement

Frank E Cahill

American Ink Paperbacks

Transitions In Retirement – Part 1

Now Available
**Parts 2 and 3 in Individual Volumes or
All 3 Parts in one Volume**
As paperbacks or ebooks at Amazon and other retailers

ISBN-10: 1548162701
ISBN-13: 978-1548162702

ALSO BY FRANK E CAHILL

Visit AmericanInkPaperbacks.com for more details and excerpts.
Available as paperbacks or eBooks at Amazon and other retailers.

Malfeasance In Office

Fifty years after the theories of Communism were published by Karl Marx the United States began a long and steady drift toward socialist principles. Instead of protecting the Constitution, American progressive idealists steered the Country away from it and into the clutches of socialized leadership. The first and biggest leap came with the adoption of the progressive income tax system implemented by the Sixteenth Amendment in 1913. It was the single largest fracture of American freedom.

Have career politicians replaced government by the people with government by the political class? Return with the author to the days of America's founders for their opinions.

This book is the basis for *The Core Question* book of essays.

The Core Question

A dozen questions that sharply divide Americans today are considered in this collection of essays. A reference copy of the US Constitution is provided for comparison. The subject matter ranges from the basic ideas of freedom as provided in the Constitution, to the transformation of America into a hybrid mixture of capitalist and socialist elements ruled by a governing class.

This companion piece to *Malfeasance In Office* offers arguments for Congressional and Supreme Court term limits, for Constitutional requirements for a balanced budget, controls on human resource spending, and a motion to repeal the Sixteenth Amendment to eliminate the progressive income tax.

The Magic of Flying

Sweeping new changes in aviation medical rules by the Federal Aviation Administration mean unprecedented opportunities to learn to fly with only a driver license. Learn about the new BasicMed Rule that opens even more flying possibilities than ever before. Read about the many levels of flying and types of aircraft that are available to the average hobbyist. Sample the thrill of the first flight lesson and learn what student pilots study in ground school.

Jake Hooter – Mail Rider

Adventures of the Pony Express for young readers aged 8 to 14. The Pony Express relied on the ability and endurance of small riders weighing less than 125 pounds. Remarkably, most of the riders were teenagers.

Jake Hooter was one of these youngsters in this historical novel for young readers that includes horses, wild animals, Indian attacks, boiling summers, and freezing blizzards. Jake endures these extreme hardships and more.

Loaded with illustrations in each chapter, this book for young readers mixes high adventure with rousing stories of actual historical events.

FOR RETIREES

Both those who have made it and those who will be joining the club.

ABOUT THE AUTHOR

Raised in the Southwest United States, the author has been active in engineering and business since the 1960s. His career includes service in the US Army, engineering and accounting assignments, and senior technical management responsibilities. Hobbies are aviation and flight instruction, reading, and writing. His range of writing includes magazine articles and books covering fiction and nonfiction subjects for adults and children.

CONTENTS

\# Not part of this volume. Included with Parts 2 and 3.

Figures

Part 1

Part 2

Part 3

Not part of this volume. Included with Parts 2 and 3.

INTRODUCTION

Our lives are filled with transitions, and it seems we are constantly adjusting to a new phase. It begins with the transitions of childhood as the body grows and the young child is learning and growing at a rapid pace. Before long puberty sets in and the young teenager struggles to adapt to the challenges of a changing body and the gray area between adolescence and adulthood. One minute they live in the realm of adult behavior, but seconds later they may revert to childish conduct. It's little different for young adults as they search for the type of individual they want to be. Middle age brings more trials as the older adult attempts to adjust to more body and hormone changes. Their metabolism slows, and unless they meet the requirements of a new transition, they begin to spread and gain weight. Blood pressure goes up, the heart responds less fully, cancer may establish a foothold, and there can be loads of other transitions.

Folks who have been retired for a while know that the challenges of old age are no less difficult or demanding. In fact, transitions in retirement may be the most bewildering of all transitions as folks must adjust to changes in their income, learn new ways of managing their assets, plan for disposal of their estate, and of course, adapt to health requirements as parts of the body become disabled or stop working at all.

During my lifetime I have had the opportunity to see people trying to deal with the retirement transition. It included watching grandparents and older friends as they tried to learn and understand what the government was throwing at them, and hoping their decisions were right. A few decades of my working career included preparing income taxes for individuals. I observed tax clients as they wrestled with the different phases of their retirement. Now, I have personally been through these transitions and the maze of options and decisions the older adult has to make. Eventually I realized how many of my tax clients needed help. I started by sharing my choices through conversation, and before long they were calling me for help. So, I jotted down my notes and experiences and prepared this discussion of transitions in retirement.

The management of the discussion has been organized into three parts that occur somewhat according to age. Part 1 begins with Preparation for Retirement when most folks begin this transition around fifty-five to sixty-five years old. The second part concerns Managing Retirement Assets after they have decided to retire and occurs roughly from age sixty-two to sixty-seven. Certainly some folks retire earlier and others later according to their circumstances, but most folks plan their retirement around Social Security eligibility, which generally begins at sixty-two. The last phase of the retirement transition can occur at any age, but those who actually complete it generally take action when they reach age sixty to seventy. This would be the Estate Planning Arrangements phase, when folks make their final plans for disposition of their assets.

Before we go much farther with these discussions, it is important to establish my lack of qualifications. I am not a securities broker, financial planner, attorney, legal adviser, or any other type of professional that consults in these matters. I do still prepare income taxes for individuals and am reasonably knowledgeable about tax information. The rest of the information that I offer is based upon my actual experience with the transition phases and what I have learned while enduring the changes. And so this discussion should be viewed as a guide to what is possible, and how to make your own choices.

It all begins with Part 1 – Preparation For Retirement. Around the age of fifty, folks begin to think a little more about retiring, and they begin to wonder if they will be ready. It should start with an inventory of assets and liabilities; that is, what you own and what you owe. Begin by examining what your sources of income will be when you retire. There are generally four types of retirement income: a pension, Social Security, savings, and part-time work.

Today, there are few people with a pension that replaces more than half their working income; usually, these are government pensions or union pensions. Social Security replaces part of working income depending upon how much of the working wage was taxed, and it ranges from 92 percent of their working wage for those who paid in the minimum tax, to as little as 26 percent of their working wage for folks who have paid the most in Social Security taxes.

Depending upon whom you believe, it is estimated that half of Americans have less than $10,000 in savings for retirement. That leaves them to rely on any pension income, Social Security, and a part-time job, if necessary.

For those fortunate enough to have a retirement nest egg, they may be faced with handling tax-advantaged savings, such as their regular Individual Retirement Account (IRA), or the Roth IRA alternative, or if they have had a retirement savings plan at work, then it will be necessary to plan the management of these accounts.

After reviewing your situation with assets and liabilities you will want to begin transition planning and actually making a steady transition to retirement. If you have savings as part of your income resources, you may want to change the types of investments you have maintained during your younger working life. Basically, there are two ways to use your savings in retirement: live off your capital savings by slowly cashing it in as you need it; or, live off the income generated by your capital savings, thus never actually spending it all.

Liabilities include debts such as a home mortgage, credit card debt, and others. There are important decisions to consider when confronting the management of debt. In general, you will be more secure in retirement if you don't have debt to deal with. As you transition into a fixed income environment, you will be able to stretch your retirement dollar farther if you can eliminate using a big part of it for debt service.

There will be rollovers to consider if you have savings stored in a retirement account. Some folks have saved in a 401(k) retirement account, or some variation of it, and they will want to decide how to handle this money. In some cases, their employer may force them to withdraw their savings, and if it is not handled correctly, they can lose a lot of money through taxes, penalties, and fees.

The specter of health care looms over most folks these days. Rarely does an employer offer comprehensive health care insurance after retirement. As a result, it will be necessary to make provisions for health care choices. This can be difficult and perplexing, but by taking the options step by step, the person nearing retirement will be ready to make these choices with a fair degree of understanding.

What to do with life insurance policies may be a consideration for some people. It can be used to cover funeral costs or as a legacy for their beneficiaries. There are interesting options that may appeal to some folks nearing retirement.

The last option discussed in Part 1 concerns when to draw Social Security benefits. First of all, it is confusing to many persons, and second, it can be agonizing to decide what to do, because it involves a system of penalties and incentives. There are penalties for taking benefits early, and incentives if the retiree waits longer to begin receiving benefits; and, all this must be juggled against a prediction of the age at death. It's similar to trying to determine how much deductible to set on your car insurance. A high deductible reduces the insurance premium, but if you have a wreck, then you're out the high deductible, and vice versa for a low deductible with its sky-high premium. There is a break-even point in all of this, and the discussion of Social Security may help you make this tricky decision.

By the time you finish Part 1, it will be time to tackle the second transition phase. This is covered in Part 2 – Managing Retirement Assets. The majority of retired Americans from sixty-two to about sixty-seven will be involved in this phase. It begins with sorting through the maze of health care options, such as Medicare, TRICARE,

Veterans Administration health system, employer plans, and the one that people must be most careful in managing, the Affordable Care Act. Since the majority of retirees will be turning to Medicare for their health care insurance needs, this program is discussed in most detail.

After completing arrangements for health care insurance, the prudent retiree will want to understand a little bit about income taxes. This is important, because taxes can have a large effect on preserving the precious savings and retirement income worked for so hard. Different categories of income are taxed at different rates, so it's important that retirement income be classified in the most advantageous way. Fortunate individuals with taxable income above $25,000 if they are single, or $32,000 married, will be required to pay income tax on a portion of their Social Security benefits. Also, lucky taxpayers with tax-deferred retirement accounts, such as the IRA or 401(k), will be required to begin paying taxes on this savings each year by making the Required Minimum Distribution amount each year. And wealthy taxpayers who earn more than $85,000 per year (single) or $170,000 (married) and have Medicare health insurance will be required to pay a larger premium than folks with lower retirement incomes.

Once you have a grasp of the basics of income taxes, it will be necessary to decide how to manage your income investments. Even if you have a small amount in savings, how you decide to manage your savings can have an important impact on your retirement income. Every little bit helps, and a minimal understanding of investing principles can make it easier.

As previously mentioned, there are different tax treatments for different categories of income. In general, the tax rates on wages and interest are different from the tax rates on qualified dividends and long-term capital gains. In most cases, the tax rate on ordinary interest will be higher than the rate on qualified dividends and long-term capital gains. This means that investors that put all their savings in interest-paying securities will pay a higher tax rate on their income. So, it isn't too difficult to conclude that it can be a big advantage to put savings into securities that pay out in the form of dividends.

Securities that pay interest include investments in a regular interest-bearing bank account, Certificates of Deposit (CD), and government or corporate bonds. Some folks resort to these types of investments because they are slightly more secure, and it is very easy to withdraw their money when needed. One method used to increase the rate of return on their savings involves what is commonly referred to as an investment ladder. Take CDs for instance, by setting up a group of CDs with different years of maturity, it is possible to receive a higher interest rate on each CD by keeping a longer term, yet still have one CD come due each year, which can be viewed as having something readily available in case of emergencies. Examples of this technique are further reviewed in Part 2.

Dividend and capital gain income usually come from investments in securities such as corporate stock or mutual funds. The tax rates on these types of income can be substantially lower; it can be as low as zero but usually not higher than fifteen percent. Savvy business investors usually take all of their income in this category, and so they pay much less than someone earning ordinary wages, or an individual living off interest payments.

Stock dividends today are reasonably attractive. They range from a few percent to as much as five to seven percent. But it can be variable, and the payout can be cut according to the requirements of the Board of Directors.

For the less faint at heart, there is the buy low sell high strategy. A lot of retired workers have sunk the majority of their savings into company stocks. Their idea is to sell off portions as needed during retirement. If they sell for more than they paid, then they will have a tax bill on the difference, a gain. If they sell for less than they paid, then they may have a tax deduction on the difference, a loss. But this can be even more variable than holding stock for the dividends. Just about everyone is familiar with the wild swings of extraordinary highs and lows in the stock market. For the retiree, a downward turn in the market could occur when they need ready cash, but a lot of their portfolio value has temporarily gone up in smoke. Still, this is a common method used by retired investors.

Mutual funds are a method used to mitigate some of the effects of market fluctuations. The operative word is mitigate, not eliminate. Mutual funds are simply a collection of investments put together in trust by a company of professional investors that is meant to diversify and reduce the effect of market fluctuations. The array of options can be paralyzing to a new investor, but a little bit of research can quickly reduce the mystery. Many mutual funds invest in a combination of corporate stocks and bonds that are meant to be more stable while providing regular dividends. A lot of these funds are designed for retired folks, and so they pay a fixed amount month after month. These funds usually pay a higher rate than regular CDs or corporate bonds.

With all the preparations completed in Part 1, and having learned to manage health care, taxes, and their retirement income in Part 2, then most retired folks will want to begin Estate Planning Arrangements as described in Part 3. Most individuals start thinking seriously about estate planning when they are between the ages of sixty and seventy. A few start at an earlier age, particularly those with large estates, while others may wait until later in making preparations for the distribution of their estate after death.

Estate planning will require you to organize your assets and liabilities. For those who did the inventory described in Part 1, the job will already be partly complete. Nevertheless it's still a tiresome job, but it can be necessary to reduce the burden on a family left behind.

Usually the first question about estate planning is how much the taxes will be. For those with small estates, let's say less than $5.49 million, there won't be any estate tax. It's easy to see that this is most people. For the lucky people with estates larger than this, then there will be taxes due, but the taxes due are paid by the estate – not the recipients of estate property.

The majority of people who make estate arrangements will want to prepare about five documents to take care of various situations as they grow older, perhaps infirmed, and after their death. They will want one or more of the following: a Revocable Living Trust, a Will, a Durable Power of Attorney, an Advance Directive for Health Care, and a Health Insurance Portability and Accountability Act (HIPAA) Waiver.

A Revocable Living Trust is merely a directive to establish how your property will be managed and distributed during your lifetime and death. It can be changed or revoked at any time you wish, should your circumstances or wishes change. It is not a substitute for a Will, so it is recommended that most people have both.

The Will is the instrument that is used to designate who receives property at death. If there is no Living Trust, then the Will must be reviewed in court to verify its accuracy and legitimacy. This can be extremely costly to the beneficiaries, and thus the recommendation for establishing a Living Trust, which avoids the court procedures and preserves assets and privacy for all concerned. If there is a Living Trust, then the Will is used as a backup to identify property that may not have been included in the Trust Assets.

The next three documents are meant for situations where retired persons have become incapacitated and can no longer make decisions for themselves. In each case the effectiveness of these documents is usually restricted until an attending physician, or a group of physicians, has prepared a statement certifying that the principal person is in fact incapacitated. The lead document is the Durable General Power of Attorney. It is simply a document to appoint someone to act on your behalf to take care of items ranging from finances and investments, to registering your car.

For those who want to exercise their right to make their own decisions regarding their health care treatment, the Advance Directive for Health Care is used to establish their demands. Again, once their condition is certified by their attending physician, then the Advance Directive establishes requirements to avoid treatment that might unduly prolong the dying process. This is important to many individuals today. In support of the Advance Directive is the HIPAA

Waiver. Although not always needed, it is comforting to have one just in case of the restrictions of rules and regulations. The HIPAA law is the one that restricts the release of health care records to unauthorized persons. This waiver removes this restriction on physicians, hospitals, and your health care agent.

Today, when faced with the high cost of attorney fees, more people are deciding to make up and execute these documents themselves. For most people they are relatively simple. The forms are repetitive, and many attorneys simply turn the process over to a legal assistant that draws up the papers using computer software, and then with very little oversight the papers are signed and a substantial fee collected. A simple Living Trust usually can set you back about $1,800, but usually they run $2,000 or more, depending on where you live. That's a big chunk out of retirement resources, and the majority of retirees simply don't have that kind of money to spare. But preparing your own legal documents is surely not for everyone. Some folks have complicated situations that require specialized documents that need to be created under the guidance of a competent lawyer. Lots of other people simply can't understand the process, and so they should seek legal help. Nowadays it is common to find elder law representatives to help those in this situation.

For the adventurous readers, there are descriptions and directions for preparing the simpler forms of legal documents. Common examples are provided in the Appendices to Part 3. Review them and decide for yourself if preparing your own legal documents is something you would like to do.

After reading Parts 1, 2, and 3, all of your questions won't be answered. There will be dozens of decisions to make, some difficult, and some perplexing. You will likely require more research and reading. Today, the Internet is a ready source of information, and there are other books and individuals to help answer your questions. But by using this guide you are started thinking about what is possible and what your next steps will be for your retirement transition.

PART 1
PREPARATION FOR RETIREMENT

After working for most of their adult lives there comes a time for everyone when they realize that time for retirement is approaching. It can be thrilling for some and drudgery for others. Regardless of attitude, those who expect to leave the workforce will want to begin planning.

Roughly ten to fifteen years before joining the retirement community, it's a good idea to begin preparations. This ranges from evaluating assets and debt that must be dealt with during retirement, to plotting the actual transition.

Part 1 provides an outline for gathering information and considering the changes that must be made, not only to make the transition as painless as possible, but also to avoid crippling mistakes that can diminish the critical resources that are so important to the pleasure of retirement.

INVENTORY ASSETS AND LIABILITIES

Somewhere around the age of fifty it is time to begin thinking about retirement. Prudent planners will start to wonder if they will have enough, and how long they will have to work in order to be prepared. The natural place to start is to evaluate what assets and liabilities have been accumulated. Now is the time to make the first list.

Write down every bank account, estimate the worth of clothing, household possessions, vehicles, tools, jewelry, books, antiques, and everything that seems important. Then the depressing part is to make note of liabilities, such as an outstanding mortgage, credit card debt, loans, and obligations that must be satisfied by paying them off or liquidating assets in order to meet the terms of the debts. Add up the value of all the assets, and then the demands of all liabilities. By subtracting the total debts from the total assets, the degree of solvency can be determined. If total assets exceed total liabilities, then the result is a solvent financial situation. If the reverse is true, then a person's financial outlook is insolvent when more is owed, in terms of liabilities, than what is owned in assets. An example of how to do this is shown in Figure 1. After preparing a list of assets and liabilities, the potential retiree in the example can see their net worth by subtracting total liabilities of $137,000 from total assets of $381,950 to arrive at $244,950 in the black; they're solvent. This type of worksheet not only helps with planning for retirement income resources, but also for reference when preparing estate documents like a living trust or will.

List of Assets and Liabilities				
Assets	Est Value	**Liabilities**		Est Value
Residence - House and Real Estate	$ 150,000	Home mortgage		$ 95,000
Bank Checking Account	$ 750	Credit card balance due		$ 14,000
Bank Savings Account	$ 2,500			
Company 401(k) Account	$ 85,000			
Life Insurance Policy Cash Value	$ 75,000			
Death Benefit ($100,000)				
Car	$ 15,000	Car loan		$ 13,000
Pickup	$ 18,000	Truck loan		$ 15,000
Boat	$ 1,200			
Personal clothing and jewelry	$ 3,500			
Household goods and furniture	$ 21,000			
Shop tools	$ 4,500			
Guns and Miscellaneous	$ 5,500			
Total Assets	$ 381,950		Total Liabilities	$ 137,000
Net Worth (Total Assets - Liabilities)	$ 244,950 **SOLVENT**			

Figure 1 - List of Assets and Liabilities

In circumstances where a person is insolvent, then a plan should be formulated to pay off the debts. It will be important to decide whether this can be accomplished before retirement or if the debts may carry into retirement. Naturally it is preferable to eliminate all debts before retirement, because the load of debt service can seriously affect the suitability of retirement income.

One exception to be considered is a home mortgage. Some people want to retire the mortgage when they stop working. It's one less drain on their income. Others, on the other hand, may have a low-interest-rate loan, and so instead of paying off the mortgage with their savings, they invest the money to earn income at a higher rate than the mortgage rate. As a result, they make a small profit on the deal. The catch is to be sure to actually invest the money, and to do it with low-risk investments.

After the list of assets and liabilities has been compiled, it is time to consider the sources of income that will be available to support retirement. There are usually four or five sources of income for the average worker. These may include a pension, Social Security benefits, personal savings, an annuity, and part-time work. Not everyone will be lucky enough to have all of these resources, while some may have even more, such as inheritances, royalties, and small business income. Whatever the situation, make an estimate of what will be available for retirement and begin considering what this will mean to the timing of when to retire.

In the introduction to this subject it was stated that more than half of Americans have less than $10,000 in savings for retirement. But this should not be overlooked. It can be very important during retirement, and with some degree of planning, it could even grow during the retirement years. For example, consider that a household needs an income of about $30,000 a year, or about $2,500 a month, during retirement. Obviously, the $10,000 in savings won't last long if the retirees draw it out when they stop working. But consider what could happen if they invest the money to make five percent. It would earn $500 a year until they retire, so their nest egg is increased. Then if they use only the interest on the $10,000 savings during retirement, they will have $500 more each year.

For those with enough resources to have saved more than $10,000, let's say $100,000, then the annual income at five percent jumps to $5,000. This could be a big help. The options are interesting, and each retired person must decide how to handle their savings. More tips on the subject are included in the review of Transition Planning in a following section.

PENSIONS AND TAX-DEFERRED SAVINGS

One of the vanishing sources of retirement income is the defined-benefit pension. This is a remnant of preceding generations where employers paid for an annuity for each employee in order to encourage employee retention. If workers remained with the company for the majority of their working lives, say twenty-five to forty years, then they were rewarded with a cash payout during their nonworking life until they died. It was a fine plan for those who stayed the course. But there were problems. First of all, if an individual left a company after a few years, they usually lost this benefit. It was called vesting, and if the employee was not vested, then this benefit was lost; and worse, at the next place of employment, it was necessary to start a new vestment period all over again. As a result, a lot of these people were left with nothing to fall back on when they retired. The second problem was that not everyone was fortunate enough to work for a company that offered retirement benefits. Companies that offered retirement plans were usually large and profitable, such as automobile companies, financial companies, utility companies, railroad companies, and the government. For folks that were self-employed, or worked for small or less profitable outfits, they were left out in the cold at retirement time.

There are still defined-benefit plans, but they are usually pared down considerably when compared to the retirement pensions of the past. It all started about forty years ago when the Individual Retirement Arrangement (IRA) was created in 1974 as part of the Employee Retirement Income Security Act. The IRA was originally meant for those employees not covered by employment-based plans. This would be the folks that didn't have the good fortune to work for big companies with big benefits and had no retirement plan at all. The Act was passed with little fan fare, and it went more or less unnoticed.

About four years after the IRA program was started, Congress expanded the provisions for personal retirement plans when Subsection 401(k) of the Internal Revenue Service Code was enacted in 1978. This provision extended tax-deferred savings plans to private companies and their employees, to be used as defined-contribution pension plans that today are commonly called 401(k) retirement plans.

Both the IRA and 401(k) were obscure and overlooked for years. Then, in 1981 the IRA provisions were extended to all qualifying individuals. This time there was more publicity, and some folks began to take notice of the IRA and its promises of tax deferral; nevertheless, participation remained sparse. But the first 401(k) plan was initiated in the same year, and employers slowly began to notice the savings in corporate overhead by phasing out the costly defined-benefits plans and replacing them with the 401(k) idea. Companies could make matching contributions to each employee's individual savings plan, which would cost less, and with less long-term commitment, than maintaining complicated annuities. As a result, the company-paid retirement plans were slowly phased out over the next twenty or so years as they were replaced with tax-deferred savings plans.

Today, most employers expect their workers to assume responsibility for their own retirement through a consistent savings plan. Some lucky employees still have generous defined-benefits pensions, but there are comparatively few. Less fortunate employees still receive a company-paid pension that is a shadow of the pensions that were common in the first part of the Twentieth Century. These companies aren't being cheap; in fact, such companies are accepting an active role in retirement income for their employees. The least fortunate, and probably the majority of employees, have no company-sponsored retirement plan and are expected to provide for themselves by utilizing Social Security, personal savings, and part-time work if needed.

Typical companies today expect their employees to have sources of income from Social Security, personal savings, and some long-term company support through a modest company-paid pension plan. The company-paid plan of today will likely replace not more than 15 percent of the worker's pre-retirement income. Coupled with estimates that Social Security will replace at least 25 percent of their income, then personal savings, such as the 401(k) is expected to make up their remaining retirement needs.

This history and evolution of pension plans and retirement savings affects most people born after 1940. So when evaluating sources of income when preparing for retirement, these folks are likely to list an IRA, 401(k), or some similar tax-advantaged retirement plan.

But there's more. The tax-advantaged retirement plan has evolved substantially since the first act of 1974. Commonly there are two types of tax-advantaged plans today called the Traditional and Roth. When the first IRA idea was implemented the amount saved was deducted from the individual's income tax statement, and the tax on this savings was deferred until the saver decided to withdraw the savings. An added benefit was extended to the income developed by the savings, such as interest, dividends, and capital gains. This income on savings was not taxed until withdrawal, also.

Then Senator William Roth of Delaware proposed an alternative idea in the Taxpayer Relief Act of 1997. His plan eliminated the tax savings on money put in an IRA, that is, there was no tax deferral and the saver paid tax on the money saved to an IRA; but, the benefit comes at withdrawal, when all tax on the income earned from the savings is available tax free. Now two types of IRA were available, so in order to distinguish one from the other, the original plan is referred to as the *Traditional IRA*, and the later version is called the *Roth IRA*. The idea caught on and was extended to 401(k) plans, too; so, today employees and retirees must understand and deal with both *Traditional 401(k)* and *Roth 401(k)* plans as well.

Variations of the 401(k) and IRA have been implemented to cover different categories of workers. They have similar names such as the 403(b) tax-advantaged retirement plan for public education organizations and some non-profit employers; the 457(b) tax-advantaged retirement plan for government and certain non-government employees; and, the 401(a) tax-advantaged retirement plan by government institutions as a retention incentive for key employees. Similarly, extended IRA programs include SIMPLE IRAs, which is the abbreviation for Savings Incentive Match Plan for Employees, and SEP, which stands for Simplified Employee Pension plan. The SIMPLE IRA is an employer-provided plan for smaller employers with no more than 100 employees that offers simpler and less costly administration rules. The SEP is similar to the Traditional IRA, but with different rules for self-employed individuals. If the self-employed person has employees, then all employees must receive the same benefits under the SEP plan as the business owner.

It's important to know what type of savings plan makes up the retirement saving portfolio. Many people may have a combination of different types of retirement savings plans, so it is important to know which types and the basic rules for handling them. A person can easily have a 401(k), a Traditional IRA, a Roth IRA, and a SIMPLE IRA, with a 457(b) mixed in for good measure. Regardless of the situation, it will be important to know how to manage one or more accounts, and what the rules will be during retirement.

Almost all retirement plans are either tax deferred at the time of the employee contribution to the plan, or are not tax deferred at the time of contribution. Besides the fact that there is an immediate tax savings during the year the tax-deferred contribution is made, there is a substantial difference in the rules for withdrawal of the savings. Regardless of the type of plan, the cardinal rule is do not touch this money unless absolutely necessary. The penalties can be severe, and the money may be a later salvation during retirement.

First, the traditional style. Money may not be withdrawn from this account before the owner is 59½-years-old without paying a tax penalty. In most cases the penalty is 10%. So, if the owner is in a 15% tax bracket for federal tax and a 5% tax bracket for state tax, and withdraws $10,000 subject to penalty, then the owner must pay $1,500 federal income tax, $500 state income tax, and $1,000 federal early withdrawal penalty. It works out like this:

Withdrawal Amount	10,000
Federal Tax at 15%	1,500
State Tax at 5%	500
Federal Penalty at 10%	1,000
Total Tax & Penalty	3,000
Net take home	7,000

It's easy to see how important it is to properly manage withdrawals from one of these accounts. After age 59½, the owner doesn't pay the penalty, but the taxes still apply.

Another part of the traditional style account that must be carefully managed is the Required Minimum Distribution (RMD). This is a minimum withdrawal that must be removed from the account each year after the owner reaches age 70½. The required amount is calculated based upon the value of the account at the end of each year and an age expectancy factor established by the IRS. The retiree may withdraw more than this amount, but is *required* to withdraw the minimum amount after reaching the RMD age. More implications of this requirement are reviewed in Part 2.

The alternative type of retirement savings account is the Roth designation. Because the account owner has already paid the income tax on the Roth contribution, the *original* direct contribution may be withdrawn at any time without income tax or penalty. The *earnings* on the saver's contribution may be taken from the account without tax or penalty if the owner is at least age 59½ and it has been at least five years since the *initial* contribution to the Roth account was made. So, if the owner waits five years and has attained the minimum age, then the income from this account will be tax free for life. If a withdrawal does not meet these requirements, then the owner must pay the ten percent penalty.

Another nice feature of the Roth account is that there is no RMD to worry about. The tax on the savings has been paid, and there is no tax on the earnings from the savings, so the Roth account is somewhat worry free after retirement.

After the inventory of sources of income, assets, and liabilities is complete, then the next step in preparing for retirement will be to plan and organize for the transition to retirement.

TRANSITION PLANNING

Planning for the transition to retirement should begin around age fifty-five, if not sooner. About this time the person nearing retirement will want to make decisions on sources of income, debt, rollovers, health care, life insurance, and Social Security. None of these questions are difficult in themselves, but the complicating factor is life expectancy. Everyone must honestly evaluate how long their retirement will last, and use this information to make these decisions. Life expectancy becomes the troubling uncertain feature.

For those with retirement savings, it must be decided whether to live off the savings by using it up slowly through retirement, or to live off the earnings from savings. Debt must be carefully examined. The future retiree must determine which debts can be paid off, and when this will be accomplished. Other decisions will be necessary for those with tax-deferred retirement savings; such as, will it be necessary to roll over funds or to convert the character of savings.

Health care considerations loom over most retirees. A dependable and affordable source of health insurance is virtually a must for nearly everyone. Requirements for health care are unavoidable, as each person must deal with the problems of an aging body, and eventual death. All wish for good health in retirement, but those who must face common ailments such as high blood pressure, joint trouble, diabetes, heart problems, and cancer, must turn to reliable health insurance for assistance.

Life insurance is another consideration. Will the benefits of life insurance be needed to pay for burial expenses, or will life insurance benefits be used as a legacy for family left behind? For those who have avoided the purchase of life insurance, should this be a consideration during the transition years?

Finally, the largest, and most agonizing question for folks as they begin to think about retirement is when to begin drawing Social Security benefits. There's a penalty for starting payments early, and a bonus for delaying the start of benefits. It's a worrisome question that can cost a few nights' sleep. There's no right answer, though, and all new retirees must weigh their own situation to decide their best course of action.

Income

So back to the beginning and planning to deal with retirement savings. If there are no retirement savings, now is the time to begin savings. Each person must save like never before. Later, the impact of savings, even at this late date in life, can have a huge impact on the quality of retirement.

For those who already have retirement savings, it will be time to consider how to use the savings during retirement. As previously discussed, will they simply use up the savings, or try to live off the income from it? Many folks try to live off the income from Certificates of Deposit (CD) with their local bank. It's not a bad idea, but most people do it because they don't know what else to do with their money. It worked well for many retirees in the days of high interest rates, but today, with some exceptions like jumbo deposits of enormous amounts, there is little interest available from CDs.

The equation is fairly simple for retired people who plan to live off their savings until it's depleted. Consider a comparison of three different cases of $2,500, $25,000, or $100,000 in a savings account. If the plan is to retire at age sixty-five and live for twenty more years, then the arithmetic is straightforward. In the first instance, the individual will have $125 a year to spend until age 85; that is $2,500 divided by 20 years equals $125 a year. Similarly, case two will have $1,250 per year, and the most fortunate of the three can spend $5,000 a year to stretch over the 20-year period.

If they earn a little in interest each year, then there'll be a little more available. Obviously, if any of them live more than 20 years, then the retirement income will be reduced in the final years of life. Simple – but troubling.

An alternative for folks who want to keep it simple could be the annuity. These are retirement plans offered by insurance companies, and in many cases, these are similar to mechanisms used by companies to provide defined-benefit pensions to their employees. In its simplest form, a person seeking retirement income pays an amount to the insurance company, which uses the money in return for a guaranteed payout to the buyer when they decide to receive benefits. Like most deals, time becomes the important aspect. The more time that elapses between paying money in and withdrawing money, the larger the payout. The sooner the annuity is purchased, the higher the annual payouts will be, and conversely, retirement benefits will be larger according to how long they are delayed.

So back to the three cases just reviewed. If their situations are noted around age 55, then each of these individuals could purchase an annuity and have something like ten years to accumulate a higher income. Even if they were age 65 it isn't too late. These folks can purchase annuities and begin receiving annual benefits right away. Predictably, these will be minimal payments, and may not be attractive at all. But, at least it is a possibility for those interested.

There are trade offs for every situation. The annuity is no different. First, there are sales charges to consider. These are not readily apparent, and potential investors should make certain to be informed. In general, the retired investors are paying the insurance company to manage their assets for them for the rest of their lives. The second characteristic is that the initial amount invested is usually used up, depending upon the plan that is chosen. There could be something left when someone dies early, but usually all of the money paid into the annuity is used up by those who live out the terms of the contract.

The appeal is for persons who don't want to fool with

managing their savings. They're willing to pay financial companies to take care of it for them. In return, they usually can depend upon a set monthly amount for the rest of their lives. They just bought a pension.

A third type of saver is the kind that wants to manage their savings themselves. These are the citizens that choose to invest in securities such as CDs, bonds, stocks, mutual funds, or other types of investments that they expect to grow in value or to payout dividends during retirement. It is their plan to live off the cash income from their investments, or to cash their investments and live off the appreciated value of their portfolio. When these investors approach the age of 55, it is about time to decide their course of action and begin the transition of their portfolio for retirement.

Younger securities investors usually maintain a collection of investments that they expect to grow in value, such as a common stock. They buy stock in a company when they are in their 20s or 30s and expect it to be worth much more when they reach retirement. But the stock market can take some wild swings, so the value of their common stock may do the same. So, as a method of protection, they will keep a little reserve invested in what they see as safer places. They may keep it in savings, CDs, or less risky mutual funds. Depending on each person's tolerance for risk and the sometimes stomach-churning periods when it seems the bottom has fallen out of the stock market, it is common for younger investors to keep around thirty percent in reserves. Their portfolio might be called a 70/30 mix; that is, 70% invested in aggressive growth stocks, and 30% in fixed income reservoirs like a savings account.

By the time investors near their 50s, they may want to begin a slow transition from aggressive to less risky. At this time many begin to adjust their investments to what is often called a balanced mix. A balanced portfolio is simply an adjustment to about 60/40. Now, they have less risk in the volatile securities, and have parked not quite half of their remaining savings in what are termed less risky investments. Clearly though, nothing is without risk, but the idea is to begin shifting into fixed income investments. They still have a majority in the stock market, but they're young enough to recover if it takes a strong and long turn downward.

A last adjustment may occur between the ages of 55 to 65, or some similar period. Here the investor begins to adjust the mix to something like 30/60/10 by retirement time. This means leaving 30% in somewhat aggressive investments, 60% in more secure fixed income types, and about 10% in cash money market or savings accounts. Some start their retirement with this mix. Others convert virtually everything to fixed income. In effect, they are doing the job of the annuity insurance company and saving the management commissions.

This can be a rewarding way to manage savings and income. It is not uncommon for retired investors to receive at least 5% or more in income on their money. So back to the three cases reviewed earlier, if each one held investments that paid the five percent income, then these investors would receive about the same income each year as if they simply cashed in their money over twenty years. The difference is that they would retain their savings as long as they live, and it could grow somewhat over the twenty years to provide higher income.

Regardless of the choices each person makes, it could be important to them to consider the options, seek more information, and begin the transition to support their plan. After deciding what the income resources will be, and what transition will be made, the person involved in the Part 1 phase will be ready to consider the disposition of their debt.

Debt
If possible, it is usually preferable for the new retiree to enter into the nonworking life with no debt. Credit cards should become and remain things of the past. If student loans linger, then every effort should be made to remove this anchor from around the neck. Car loans should be paid off, and the best part of a home mortgage paid off if the retired person owns a home.

Each person should have lined up their debts during the inventory of assets and liabilities. Additionally, each debt should be listed according to interest rate. It should make sense to pay off the highest interest rates first. In most cases this will be credit card or car loan debt. So part of the pre-retirement planning should be to decide how many years are left until retirement, and then how much must be dedicated to each debt to eliminate it.

Starting with the credit cards. If it is a substantial amount, then stop using the credit cards and eliminate all but one card. A substantial amount will mean different things to different people. In general, if the credit card debt amount exceeds 10% of annual pay, then it may be problematic; for example, $3,000 or more outstanding debt for a person earning $30,000 is quite a bit; similarly, $10,000 can be quite a burden for a person earning $100,000 each year. Take a look at the interest for each year. Ten percent of the unpaid balance in these cases can add up to $300 to $1,000 a year. This will be a considerable drain on a reduced retirement income. So gather up the cards. Find the cheapest rate and then pay off all the other cards with the cheaper card, and set up a plan to pay off that card by retirement time. If it's $3,000 total debt and ten years to retirement, then plan to pay out over $300 a year until it's gone. And, don't use the card for purchases that can't be paid off at the end of the month. Without this discipline, retired individuals will begin retired life with a major drain and worry.

If a fancy car is a goal during retirement, then now is the time to plan and save for it. Don't take out an expensive car loan just before retirement, unless it is in the budget and can be afforded. The better way is to pay off the current car before retirement, and then save money for a different one when a replacement is needed. If a late model used car will work, then save the depreciation and buy a good used car with cash, if possible. The savings will be terrific as can be seen in Figure 2. The example assumes a 7-year loan at 5% interest to purchase a new car for $30,000. A down payment of $1,500 is part of the example. The first column shows each year after the car was bought new. The estimated depreciation of the car is demonstrated in the next column, and the third column shows the declining value of the car in each year. Lost value of the car in depreciation is roughly $21,858. The remaining balance owed on the loan is seen in the fourth column. Notice that the amount owed on the car is more than the value of the car for the first few years, which is common for many auto loans; and, unfortunately, this is exactly when patrons decide to trade it in to repeat the process. After making the down payment and paying $4,925 a year for seven years, the buyer has paid $35,975 for the car. The total cost of the car, then, is $5,975 for interest plus $21,858 lost value to depreciation, which totals $27,833; that's about $3,976 a year for transportation, not including fuel and maintenance.

Cost of New Car Depreciation and Financing					
Year	Depr	Value	Owed	Paid	Interest
New		30,000	28,500	1,500	-
1	5,100	24,900	25,000	4,925	1,425
2	4,233	20,667	21,324	4,925	1,250
3	3,513	17,154	17,465	4,925	1,066
4	2,916	14,237	13,413	4,925	873
5	2,420	11,817	9,158	4,925	671
6	2,009	9,808	4,691	4,925	458
7	1,667	8,142	0	4,925	232
Totals	21,858			35,975	5,975
Notes:	Down payment of $1,500				
	Finance $28,500 for 7 years at 5% interest				

Figure 2 - Cost of New Car Depreciation and Financing

Retirees wanting to save a few bucks on car expenses might save their money in order to pay cash for the car when it is three or four years old. At age three the car could be bought for around $17,154, saving $12,846 in depreciation. The cost for owning the same car with this strategy is the cost of depreciation for the last four years, which works out to about $2,253 per year, plus the fuel and maintenance.

Naturally it isn't a new car, but how long does a new car feel new? After about six months for most motorists, they begin thinking about the next loan.

Student loan debt remaining at retirement may seem silly, but these things have a way of lingering. For sure, they saddle young kids with a grudging debt service, but many middle-aged adults take on student loans to pursue a new degree, and the debt can be substantial. The loans are easy to get but not so easy to pay off. The interest rate isn't generous, and if possible, this debt should be eliminated before quitting the work place.

The home mortgage is not so easy. It can be a huge number that simply can't be paid off by retirement time. On the other hand, some folks plan to keep the mortgage rather than paying it off, and then they invest the money to build retirement income. Other people decide to sell out and rent, or buy a smaller home with no mortgage, or a smaller mortgage. Those who plan to rent should be sure their retirement income will cover rental expenses comfortably. The same is true for individuals who decide on a smaller place. Closing costs can be substantial and should be figured into the budget.

It sounds nice to be free of a mortgage, and it is probably a sound decision for most people. Pay it off and be free of the drain of the monthly payment. But the budget should include taxes in this situation, and a reserve for future necessities such as a new roof, a new furnace, or other major maintenance necessities. A simple plan is to place some of the original mortgage payment into a reserve savings and let it build for the eventual need for it. If all of the mortgage savings is used as retirement income, then the homeowner may have a financial crisis later; and, perhaps a new, smaller mortgage to pay for repairs.

Bolder home owners who have plenty of money in reserve to pay off their mortgage sometimes use a tactic to keep paying the mortgage and putting the reserve in income-producing investments. Think about a homeowner with about $50,000 left on the mortgage and more than $50,000 saved up. When they obtained their mortgage they were fortunate enough to borrow at 3.5%, and their monthly payment is about $400 a month, or $4,800 a year. They decide to put the $50,000 in five different mutual funds that are expected to pay eight percent, or $4,000 a year. Roughly speaking, they are using the interest they earn on their investments to pay the interest and part of the principle on their home. When the home is paid off, they will still have $50,000 supporting their income, and have accrued the $50,000 in home equity. Their plan is workable, but there are a couple of risks. One pitfall is that their investment does not pay the rates they expected. Another is that they don't invest at all and spend the money on other things. Their plan isn't a bad plan, but only the most disciplined financial manager should try it. Those in doubt should probably pay off the mortgage and enjoy being debt free.

A summary of a debt analysis is presented in Figure 3. This can be used as an example to set up a personal plan to eliminate personal debts.

Debt Analysis			
Type	Amount	Rate	Annual Payment
CreditCo Card Balance	2,000	19.0%	380
DebtCo Card Balance	6,400	18.0%	1,152
PayCo Card Balance	7,300	16.0%	1,168
Total Credit Card	15,700	17.2%	2,700
EasyAuto Car Loan	4,600	5.0%	230
EdCo Student Loan	2,500	4.0%	100
HomeEc Mortgage	50,000	3.5%	1,750
Total Other Loans	57,100	3.6%	2,080
Total Debt	72,800	6.6%	4,780

Figure 3 - Debt Analysis

In the example the person near retirement has accumulated some typical debts. There are three credit card balances, which add up to $15,700 with annual payments of

$2,700. As expected, the credit card interest rates are highest, ranging from 16% to 19% and averaging about 17.2% for the three of them. In addition, the prospective retiree owes on a car loan, a student loan, and a home mortgage, which total $57,100 as indicated in the figure. It all adds up to $72,800 requiring annual interest payments of $4,780, which works out to a total debt rate of about 6.6% (4,780 / 72,800). This situation needs to be modified before retirement day, if possible.

Clearly, the credit card debt and use needs to go. One method would be to consolidate all of them into the cheapest rate, but it is still high and subject to change according to the whims of the credit card company. Another option might be a second mortgage, but it will be important to find a loan with a low interest rate. The 3.5% rate of the current mortgage may not be attainable, but perhaps something is available for less than the other rates.

In lieu of the second mortgage, there are low-rate loans available that could be used to pay off these debts. If a rate can be obtained that is lower than the rate on most of these debts, then this could be a viable option.

Every effort should be made to clear the debts other than the mortgage. A second job might be a good option to retire as much debt as possible. If downsizing is part of the retirement plan, then it might make sense to sell off unnecessary possessions to pay off accumulated debt.

Rollovers

How to handle Individual Retirement Arrangement (IRA) or 401(k) retirement savings is the next chore during transition planning. For those who don't have a retirement savings account there is nothing to worry about. But most people will have a little something saved back from their years of hard work. How to handle a 401(k) or an IRA is not difficult, but there are some rules to understand before making changes. It's important to understand that all dealings with these accounts are done with the trustee, or custodian, of the account; not the employer, and it's equally important that directions are clear.

First, the 401(k). Many companies and trustees now allow employees and retirees who have left the company to leave the account with the trustee. This means that the account holder may be restricted on how they can invest their savings. A given trustee may offer a number of different mutual funds or other vehicles for saving, but they may also restrict the account owner to their own menu of investments. Fidelity, for instance, may restrict all investments in a Fidelity-based 401(k) to Fidelity-offered investments. There is not a thing wrong with that, but some investors may wish to have more options.

In some cases the retiree may be required to liquidate the 401(k) account. This also is not a problem, but it must be handled exactly right, or investors could loose a substantial portion of their retirement savings to the tax collector.

So, for folks who need to close a 401(k) because they are required to do it, or because they want more investing options, the answer is to roll it over into an IRA, and do it electronically. It's a simple matter of finding a bank or investment company that is satisfactory, and then requesting a rollover of the 401(k). The receiving company will provide transfer paper work. The investor just supplies the account information on the 401(k), and signs it. The transfer of funds occurs electronically as a rollover and is not a taxable event.

The alternative is extremely tenuous. This would involve receiving a check for the amount to be closed out. The problem occurs in that the recipient has only 60 days to open a new account, and only has part of the money. The trustee must withhold income tax, so the recipient will not have this available to rollover. Here's an example. Say a 401(k) is liquidated in the amount of $40,000. The trustee must withhold twenty percent ($8,000) and pay the recipient only $32,000. The $8,000 is gone, paid to the IRS. So, if the recipient can't come up with the additional $8,000 to roll over the entire $40,000, then they can only avoid paying taxes on the $32,000. The recipient will owe federal and state taxes on the $8,000, and if their age is under 59½ they will owe an additional 10% penalty of $800 on top of the income tax. If possible, this method should not be attempted.

Too much can go wrong that can rob the retirement nest egg unnecessarily.

For those interested in a Roth IRA (RIRA), the transfer could be made to an RIRA; however, this is a taxable event. Reconsider the $40,000 rollover just discussed. It could be possible to roll over a part of it each year for several years leading up to retirement and pay the income taxes due on it each year. The main thing is to avoid this until after age 59½ to save the early distribution penalty. Once the money is placed into an RIRA and the tax paid, then the earnings and future withdrawals during retirement will be tax free.

Some folks prefer converting to an RIRA. Some like to do it during their working years if they have a lot of disposable income to pay the taxes. Others like to wait until retirement years when their income will be lower along with their tax bracket. Consider the difference in the 15 percent and 25 percent federal tax brackets and assume similar state tax brackets of 4 and 6 percent. This means the total tax on an RIRA conversion could be 19 percent versus 31. On $40,000 the total tax difference would be $7,600 versus $12,400, which is $4,800 more.

The last thing to consider in rollovers is the SIMPLE IRA. It's important to be aware that the saver must wait two years from the date of the initial contribution into a SIMPLE IRA before it can be rolled over into another type of IRA. If this period is not honored, then a penalty may be applied.

By now, the importance of knowing the sources of retirement income and debt should be apparent. Also, it should be evident that capital, or savings, is the most important asset for retirement. Capital should be protected first and foremost. The loss of capital usually results in a loss of income. As retirement time draws nearer, the prudent person should begin to pinch pennies to preserve and build this important resource.

Health Care Insurance

With a general plan in place for maximizing income and minimizing debt, the transition planning can turn to considerations for health care insurance. Few employers offer retiree health care insurance benefits. Those that do are usually expensive or cover minimal needs. For retired Americans this leaves few choices, and Medicare is the choice for most. Retired military service personnel may turn to TRICARE, the Department of Defense health system. Other veterans may seek health care through the health system of the Veterans Administration. Low-income retirees may seek assistance from Medicaid, and Native Americans may turn to the Indian Health Service if they qualify.

The newest option for low-income Americans that are not yet eligible for Medicare is the Affordable Care Act that may offer assistance in paying the premium for health care. Qualifying as low-income is defined as households with income between 100% and 400% of the federal poverty level. It's a variable that depends upon the size of the family and household earnings. These plans are not that cheap, but they offer health care without restrictions to pre-existing conditions.

Some individuals elect self-insurance, or to simply roll the dice. Typically this occurs with people who elect to retire before reaching Medicare eligibility at age 65. Obtaining a private insurance policy on their own is an extraordinary expense. Wealthier families elect to bare the burden and buy the expensive coverage. Daring people with good health often just go without health care coverage until they reach age 65, although this option is becoming more expensive with the implementation of the Affordable Care Act and its stiff penalties for failure to obtain health care insurance. The penalty starts at $695 per adult and half that for each child under eighteen. That's a minimum penalty of $1,390 for a married couple, but it could be as much as double or higher if they have a large income.

The vast majority of retirees elect Medicare if they are old enough. The cost for new enrollees is roughly $134 per month per person. Basic Medicare covers about half of actual medical expenses, but there are supplemental options that may be selected which cost extra but provide more comprehensive coverage. More extensive discussion of Medicare and health care coverage is reviewed in Part 2 –

Managing Retirement Assets. While working through the phase of preparation for retirement, the individual approaching retirement will want to learn as much as possible about personal options and have an idea of which option will be the health care choice at retirement.

Life Insurance

Next on the planning list is life insurance. Some have it, some don't. Many wonder if they should have life insurance. Those without life insurance may be in the same boat as those with little or no savings. It can be expensive to obtain life insurance later in life, but for those who would like this benefit, the preparation-for-retirement stage is likely a better time to purchase life insurance than after retirement.

There are at least three reasons most retired adults want some sort of life insurance. They want to provide for a spouse, they want to leave a legacy for their children, and they want to cover death and burial expenses. The first two may be the most expensive options. The time element is the costly portion of a life policy for a person of advanced age. The more life expectancy and longer period to pay premiums, the lower the cost of insurance.

High income earners with substantial savings may want to consider a single premium paid up policy. They simply pay the entire cost of the policy in a lump sum. Some folks use this as a method to provide their financial legacy. They use a part of their savings to establish this benefit, then they consider the rest of their savings as theirs for retirement. It leaves a sense of freedom to use up their savings for their own situation, because the spouse or children will receive the life insurance benefit. It's a tax free option for the beneficiaries, too.

For those who are not fortunate enough to have a large savings, or who can't afford a large policy, they may decide on a burial policy. If this is the choice, then it should be included in the retirement budget. Life insurance salesmen can provide the estimated burial costs for the future, and this can be another worry solved.

Social Security

The last discussion concerning preparations for retirement is Social Security. The most perplexing element of the Social Security question is when to begin receiving benefits. Time, or life expectancy, again becomes the undetermined primary issue. By the time they reach age 62, a lot of Americans are simply out of gas. They want to quit working. Probably the main benefit of retirement is the freedom from having to be at a certain place at a certain time, and it is quite appealing to people in their 60s.

A lot of folks would like to work part-time, or phase-in to retirement, before they completely stop working. This could be a way to keep reducing debt. But if they expect to start Social Security benefits while still working, it will be important to know how much can be earned at work before Social Security benefits are reduced.

Deciding when to start Social Security is an important part of making preparations for retirement. It all begins with an understanding of the terms, "Full Benefit Retirement Age," "Early Retirement Age," and "Delayed Retirement Age."

The Full Benefit Age is the age that the Social Security Administration uses to calculate remaining life expectancy and thus the amount of benefits that each individual may receive, based upon the amount of taxes that have been collected during the working lifetime. The full retirement age was set at age 65 when the program was started around 1936. That's easy enough to understand, but then it became confusing to future retirees, because the full benefit age was changed to a different age for people born at different times. It all started in 1983 when Congress realized that the Social Security Trust Fund was in jeopardy of running out of money to meet the obligations of this national promise. As a result, several changes were made to fix the program, and one of these was a modification of the retirement age for full benefits. In order to be fair to people who were nearing retirement age, it was decided to phase in an increase in the full benefit age. The age rise started from age 65 for people born after 1936 until it reaches age 67 for folks born in 1960 and later. This effectively covers the baby boomer generation. Figure 4 is a chart showing the increase of the full benefit retirement age according to the year of birth.

So the first piece of the puzzle for each individual is to determine the effective Full Benefit Retirement Age. Once this is known, then the effect of early or delayed retirement can be determined.

Social Security Retirement Age for Full Benefits			
Year of Birth	Full Retirement Age	Year of Birth	Full Retirement Age
1937 & earlier	65	1955	66-2 months
1938	65-2 months	1956	66-4 months
1939	65-4 months	1957	66-6 months
1940	65-6 months	1958	66-8 months
1941	65-8 months	1959	66-10 months
1942	65-10 months	1960 & later	67
1943-1954	66		

Note: If born on Jan 1st of any year, refer to previous year.

Figure 4 - Social Security Retirement Age for Full Benefits

Early Retirement Age benefits are available at age 62 with a permanent reduction of the full benefit amount. For people with a full benefit age of 65 the reduction is 80 percent of the full benefit amount. This means that every $1,000 of monthly full benefit is reduced to $800 for the folks who start their Social Security at age 62. But, it's a sliding scale that's figured on a month-to-month basis. This can be seen when retirement is delayed until age 62 and 8 months, then the monthly benefit would be larger, and as expected, the amount forfeited smaller.

The early retirement benefits are still available for people who want to retire early but have a higher retirement age. For example, a person with a full benefit retirement age of 67 may retire at age 62, but the reduction in benefits will be 70 percent of the full benefits age. Thus, for these folks, each $1,000 of full retirement benefits taken at age 62 will be reduced to $700. All the same sliding scales are in effect according to the full benefits retirement age for each person and to the age at the month benefits begin.

The last nuance of the benefits program is the Delayed Retirement Age feature. As an incentive for people to wait as long as possible before starting their benefits, the payout amount can be increased for each month it is delayed after the person reaches full retirement age. This financial bonus increases until it maxes out at age 70. It increases 8 percent per year until it reaches 32 percent at age 70. This would mean that each $1,000 monthly benefit would be $1,320 if the person waited until age 70 to start receiving benefits.

It's fairly simple to understand. Retire early, get less; or, retire late and get more. The confusion is understanding the full benefit age. Once this is established, then the total focus on reductions or bonuses can be understood for each circumstance, so, after the full benefit age is known, the question is when to start.

As a general rule, early or late retirement provides about the same total benefits over a lifetime. For those who retire early, the monthly benefit amounts will be smaller to account for the longer period that benefits are received. For those who choose to retire late, the larger benefit amount will be in effect for a shorter period of time. The tormenting question is life expectancy. Plenty of folks have retired at age 62, only to live a few months. For them the answer is clear. For most, though, it isn't clear.

There is a break-even-age that occurs around age 78. This age is roughly the same regardless of the full benefit retirement age or the actual age. In other words, the break-even age for a person whose full retirement age is 66 compared to another person whose full benefit age is something different, will break even around age 78 whether they retire at age 62 or any other age between earliest possible age and full retirement age. An example of this is shown in Figure 5.

In this figure it shows a comparison between an early retirement at age 62 and one at full retirement age of 66.

Next to each age is shown the annual benefit amount. In the first case it is reduced by 25%, so the early retiree will receive $750 for each $1,000 of the full retirement benefit. The next column builds the cumulative amount received at any point. As shown at about age 78, the person who waits four years will have accumulated more benefits; it compares as $12,750 to $13,000. If these two individuals live to age 85, then the difference is $18,000 to $20,000. It should be remembered that this chart is based upon a benefit of $1,000, so it could increase by 10 to 20 times, depending upon the actual benefit amount. This means a person who is eligible for $15,000 in full benefits should multiply the differences by 15; so, at the age of 85, the cumulative difference would be $270,000 versus $300,00 in lifetime benefits.

Earliest Retirement Benefits versus Full Retirement Benefits at Age 66								
	Start at Age 62		Start at Full Age 66			Start at Age 62		Start at Full Age 66	
	Annual	Cumulative	Annual	Cumulative		Annual	Cumulative	Annual	Cumulative
Age	Amount	Amount	Amount	Amount	Age	Amount	Amount	Amount	Amount
62	750	750			74	750	9,750	1,000	9,000
63	750	1,500			75	750	10,500	1,000	10,000
64	750	2,250			76	750	11,250	1,000	11,000
65	750	3,000			77	750	12,000	1,000	12,000
66	750	3,750	1,000	1,000	78	750	12,750	1,000	13,000
67	750	4,500	1,000	2,000	79	750	13,500	1,000	14,000
68	750	5,250	1,000	3,000	80	750	14,250	1,000	15,000
69	750	6,000	1,000	4,000	81	750	15,000	1,000	16,000
70	750	6,750	1,000	5,000	82	750	15,750	1,000	17,000
71	750	7,500	1,000	6,000	83	750	16,500	1,000	18,000
72	750	8,250	1,000	7,000	84	750	17,250	1,000	19,000
73	750	9,000	1,000	8,000	85	750	18,000	1,000	20,000

Figure 5 - Earliest Retirement Benefits versus Full Retirement Benefits at Age 66

This simple chart compares only the amount of benefits received and how much of the total benefit is forfeited after the break-even point. What it doesn't consider is the additional Social Security taxes that will be paid by the individual who continues working a few more years. If these are peak earning years, then the total benefit may be increased further. Other items that have been discounted in the chart include any income that may be earned from investing some of the early retirement benefits, the effects of the annual Cost of Living Allowance that increases benefits on a more or less annual basis, or inflation factors. Few folks, though, are in a position to invest their Social Security benefits, so this chart is a general indicator for most.

For folks who want to continue working for a while after they start receiving their Social Security benefits, there is the question of how much they can earn before their benefit payment is reduced. First, there is no limitation on earnings after the full benefit age is attained. No matter when they started receiving benefits, after they reach the full benefit age, then retirees may earn as much as they want.

If a retiree begins receiving benefits before the full retirement age, then some of their benefit may be withheld if they exceed a certain amount of earnings. The reduced payments are not truly lost, though; they are withheld by the government until the retired beneficiary reaches the full retirement age. Their benefits will increase at full retirement age to account for benefits withheld due to earlier earnings.

The limitation on earnings is based upon wages and net self-employment income. Investment earnings, interest, pension and annuity payments, and capital gains are not counted as earnings when figuring the limitation. There are two base amounts that set the earnings limit: one is for folks who were under the full retirement age for the entire year, and the other for folks who were under age for part of the year. For 2017, these amounts are $16,920 and $44,880.

If individuals start benefits early and earn more than the base amount, then $1 in benefits is withheld for each $2 earned above $16,920 for people who were under full retirement age for the whole year, and $1 is held back for every $3 above $44,880 for persons working and reaching full retirement age during the same year.

Here is an example for a person who is under the full retirement age for a full year. Assume the Social Security benefit is $7,200 per year and the beneficiary earns $22,000 on the job. The $22,000 exceeds the base limit of $16,920 by $5,080 (22,000 − 16,920). In this case Social Security benefits will be reduced a dollar for every two above the limit. It would be $2,540 (5,080 / 2), and the person would receive payments of $4,660 for the year (7,200 − 2,540).

Although the withheld payments will be returned at full retirement age, it's important to consider the effect of these limitations on the total retirement plan. Those who plan to phase-in like this should check the numbers with the Social Security office for the year they want to start benefits.

So the last step in planning for retirement is to determine the full retirement age for Social Security, and then to decide when to retire, and whether to phase-in.

A lot can be accomplished in the years preceding retirement from age 55 to 65. Once the planning steps have been accomplished, then it is important to continue to review it every year or so, and make adjustments as necessary. It will be an easier task to review and adjust the inventory of the sources of income and liabilities. The battle plan for handling tax-advantaged retirement savings can be adjusted. And finally, the actual transition plan should be rechecked.

Will retirement income come from savings, and will the savings generate more income from investments? Is the balanced plan for investments still accurate, or are changes needed there? How is the plan developing to eliminate debt?

Can it be more aggressive? How about that life insurance policy and how will it be used? Will health care insurance come from Medicare or have life events changed the plan? And has the defining question for retirement changed – at what age will Social Security benefits be started?

It's a lot of work, but satisfying for those who like to be in control of such things. In the end, an organized plan can save the prudent planner retirement money and can avoid a lot of heart-breaking mistakes that can cause suffering during retirement.

Now with a plan, the potential retiree can focus on work, savings, and cheerful anticipation of retirement. When the happy day arrives, the retired planner is ready for Part 2 – Managing Retirement Assets.

www.ingramcontent.com/pod-product-compliance
Lightning Source LLC
Chambersburg PA
CBHW030548290526
45786CB00004B/1915